A Roadmap for Success: What it Takes to Build a Successful Franchise

A real world glimpse into the vital partnership between the franchisee and the franchisor

by Leslie Lautzenhiser

VOLUME 1 (EPISODES 1-10)

A Roadmap For Success: What it Takes to Build a Successful Franchise
Copyright © 2011 by Leslie Lautzenhiser
http://franchise.50interviews.com

ISBN #: 978-1-935689-12-6
First edition.
Printed in the United States of America

Published by 50 Interviews Inc.
www.50interviews.com

All rights reserved. No part of this book may be reproduced in any form or by any electronic or mechanical means, including information storage and retrieval systems, without written permission from the author, except in the case of a reviewer, who may quote brief passages embodied in critical articles or in a review.

Trademarked names appear throughout this book. Rather than use a trademark symbol with every occurrence of a trademarked name, names are used in an editorial fashion, with no intention of infringement of the respective owner's trademark.

The information in this book is distributed on an "as is" basis, without warranty. Although every precaution has been taken in the preparation of this work, neither the author nor the publisher shall have any liability to any person or entity with respect to any loss or damage caused or alleged to be caused directly or indirectly by the information contained in this book.

Original 50 Interviews concept by Brian Schwartz
Cover by Jennifer Dervaes of Jadesign

Waypoint and **Conclusion** chapters are reprinted with permission of *FranChoice, Inc. FranChoice* is a national network of consultants dedicated to helping consumers find their ideal match in a franchise business. Since 2000, *FranChoice* has helped over 6,000 people become business owners through their free service. For more information, go to **www.franchoice.com**, or call toll free 877-396-4238.

ACKNOWLEDGEMENTS

I would like to thank the following individuals for their support throughout this process:

Stephen Hogan, for mentoring me, for helping me down my path of being a franchisee, and for being a wonderful business partner and friend.

FranChoice, for their generous contributions of the Waypoint and Conclusion chapters in this edition.

Brian Schwartz, for giving me this wonderful opportunity to publish this book and for his words of encouragement throughout the process.

The wonderful men and women whose stories are contained in this book and who took the time from their busy schedules to participate in the interview process.

My family, for always supporting me through all my crazy schemes and dreams.

My friends, who are always checking in and always giving me support and encouragement daily!

My husband Stephen, for allowing me to be all that I am and supporting me always.

For my children, the reason I get out of bed, the reason I work so hard, and the reason I can love so much.

Thank you all!

FOREWORD

When Leslie asked me to write the forward for her first book I was surprised. "Why me?" I asked. Leslie has closer friends, acquaintances and business professionals she's known much longer than me. However, in her path and quest to be an entrepreneur, consultant and author, our paths are very intertwined.

It doesn't surprise me that Leslie has become a published author; she's a terrific writer in both style and content. You will find this work both absorbing and insightful. It mixes the stories of other like minded franchisee business owners with a masterful connection to the real world. This allows the reader to envision themselves mounting an investigation, gathering facts, separating the assumptions from truth and then answering the most critical questions, "Can I see myself doing this? Do I want to do this?"

I met Leslie and Stephen, her husband, as prospects through my consulting practice at FranChoice. This was in May of 2005. I don't recall if they found me or were referred by another person. I assisted in placing them as franchisees. I remember distinctly that at the start they had their minds and hearts fixed on a pizza business. In my profession this is called "franchise infatuation." When a person is struck with this mindset, they haven't looked at any facts to support an already made emotional choice. Logic is gone, "Don't bother me with the details; I'm justifying my decision."

Stephen and Leslie reflected and pondered as we documented what they wanted the ideal business to deliver for them. What life style factors were required for them to find the perfect business? They ultimately understood that it isn't what the business does, but what it will do for them. The process continued and I presented them with three wildly different franchise brands; *All American Deli, Pop-A-Lock* and *PuroClean*. They thought the first two concepts were exciting; however the phone almost went dead when I presented a fire, water and mold restoration service. All Stephen could see was crawling around water logged basements with spiders. By the way, Stephen HATES spiders! No pizza or food franchises were in the mix.

To their credit, they stuck with the due diligence process and little by little, *PuroClean* rose from last place. It ultimately became the brand they selected. Amazingly, this happens about 75% of the time. It underscores the value of two time tested mantras:

- **Take your assumptions, turn them into questions and you will find the truth.**
- **Knowledge dispels fear.**

Near the end of my franchise consulting services, Leslie asked me very directly, "What do I have to do to become a franchise consultant like you?" "Leslie, you aren't even a franchisee yet," I responded. "Prove that you are a top performing franchisee, learn the profession, and then call me when you think you're ready." So that's exactly what Leslie did! In January of 2009, Leslie embarked on an aggressive effort to learn franchise consulting. Since she's bright, determined and relentless, Leslie was ready to start working with individuals who were at life's crossroads and assist them in exploring franchises in no time!

It's been a pleasure to mentor Leslie and to see her grow in expertise, understanding and compassion. I believe her genuine qualities are reflected in her book. If you have the fortune of working with her, you will come to know a very special woman, mother and colleague.

Stephen Hogan

TABLE OF CONTENTS

Introduction i

Aaron Buche, Camp Bow Wow 1

Troy Cook, CertaPro Painters and Shelf Genie 7

Betty Corbitt, Gotcha Covered 13

Waypoint: Don't Waste your Time 21

Sarah Kruse, Seeking Sitters 25

Jim Lautzenheiser, Big O Tires and Grease Monkey 31

Waypoint: Employer or Employee? 37

Stephen Lautzenhiser, PuroClean 41

Sean McEntire, CertaPro Painters 47

Waypoint: Advantages and Disadvantages of Franchising 55

Dean & Kristin Moran, Synergy HomeCare 61

Craig Radice, Pooch-Mobile 69

Matt Swope, Heaven's Best Carpet Cleaning 75

Conclusion: First Steps 81

About the Author 85

INTRODUCTION

I distinctly remember driving around with my father in my hometown of Redding, California as a young girl and looking at all the big houses up on the hillside outside of town.

"I wonder who lives up there," I said to my father.

"I can tell you this much," he said. "They probably own their own business."

That image and those words stuck with me. They stuck with me throughout high school and college when I was pursuing my degree in Journalism. They stuck with me when I first got out of school and got my first "real job." Through my career in human resources and working for various start-ups in the Silicon Valley, those words came back to me again and again.

So it was no real surprise to me when a friend of mine from grad school asked me to start an HR consulting practice in January of 1998. I called upon those words and those images from my childhood, and I gave notice to my corporate job and started on my path of entrepreneurship.

Along the way I hit bumps. I had tremendous joy. I remember staring in pride at the sign on the door of my HR practice and thinking, "this is my business."

Once you are bitten by the entrepreneur bug, it's hard to recover. Though I briefly made my way back to a corporate job, I never forgot what if felt like to be in business for myself.

And in early 2005 when my husband and I were contemplating a move to Colorado and a major career change, I once again recalled those images and suggested the business ownership path to my husband. This time, guided by Stephen Hogan, our wonderful franchise consultant, we went down the path of a franchise business.

My husband and I are probably like many of you who will be reading this book. We knew we wanted a better life for our children. More quality time. More control over our own destiny. Having ridden the Silicon Valley roller coaster for over 15 years, my husband and I both realized that to truly be in control over our financial future, we needed to be in business for ourselves.

We chose a franchise because we understood the value in having a solid business plan that had been replicated and perfected. We knew that going into business for ourselves armed with support and a strong financial backing of the franchise parent, was good business. We would come up to speed and hit the ground running much faster, than if we had started our own business from scratch. We found a business that fit all our requirements—geographic, financial, life style.

Oh, there were some sleepless nights at first. I still remember practically peeling the envelope that contained our franchise check out of my husband's hand to put it in the mail. "Just give it to me. We're doing this," I said.

Five years later, we are running a successful restoration business in town. We have control over our future, have the flexibility we so desired, and have pride knowing this is a business we are running together and helping out our community at the same time.

Two years ago, I went back to our franchise consultant, Stephen Hogan, and told him I wanted to get into franchise consulting as well. I was so profoundly impressed by what the process had done for me and my husband, that I wanted to help others find their path. I have enjoyed learning the trade and speaking with many individuals and couples throughout the US, and have helped them determine if franchising is the right path for them. When I had the opportunity to write this book, I became very excited at the possibility of reaching out to that one person who has always wanted to be in business for themselves. The one who wasn't sure how to go about evaluating what business to get into and whether it was a fit for them.

I hope as you read the inspiring stories of the people I interviewed for this book, you might see a bit of yourself in one of them. I hope that if there is something inside of you that has always wanted to be in business for yourself, that this book will help you take the first step and will initiate a conversation and investigation that, I believe, could change your life.

Running a business is a lot of hard work. It's also very rewarding. I wouldn't change the long days or the days of stress for anything. This is where I want to be. I think I've always known it, ever since the days I saw those houses on the hill in Redding.

If you dream it, make it so.

To your success!

Leslie Lautzenhiser

1

Aaron Buche, Camp Bow Wow

INTERVIEW

Q. What franchise did you purchase and when?
A. We originally purchased the Camp Bow Wow Colorado Springs franchise in 2003. When we originally bought the franchise, we bought territory rights to the Colorado Springs market as well as the Fort Collins market. We started the Colorado Springs business in 2003, and then in 2005 we opened up our Monument location here in Colorado. Shortly thereafter, we decided to build our next location in Fort Collins, Colorado. We sold off our rights to the Colorado Springs and Monument locations to purchase the rights to Fort Collins. My wife and I are now the owners here and we have been open for four years now.

Q. When was the company founded and how many existing franchisees are there in the system?
A. The company was founded in 2003. We were actually the second franchisee to sign on. We knew that we were going to be blazing tails by getting into this franchise, but we loved the concept. There are over 100 camps now in the franchise system.

Q. Had you ever run a business before opening your franchise?
A. I had not run my own business before. I come from a family of entrepreneurs. My family owns a business that has been in the family for over 100 years, so I definitely saw firsthand what it is like owning and running a business. I had never run a business myself, however. Coming from the corporate world, the transition was really easy because I have always known I wanted to be a business owner. It was exciting and not as hard as it probably is for most.

> *"With the franchise, I was getting a partner that was going to help..."*

Q. What attracted you to a franchise concept as opposed to starting your own business from scratch?
A. Two things: The first is the help you receive with the business' policies and procedures, and what to do on a day-to-day basis. I felt confident that I could figure it out on my own, but I wanted to do it right. With the franchise, I was getting a partner that was going to help me with that. The second thing is that franchising is the way the country is moving today. People can go to any town and they look for a name they recognize and trust to do their business. I envision five or ten years down the lane hearing people say "Camp Bow Wow," and they would know and trust that name.

Q. Did you consider other franchises in your search? If so, which ones?
A. Not within the pet industry. When we were doing our research there weren't really any other viable options at the time, and we really liked this industry.

Q. What attracted you to the franchise you now run and how did you determine this was the best franchise for you?
A. I knew that this was a business where I would love to show up to work every day. I wanted a customer service experience. I knew that I would be good at dealing with both pets

and their owners. As a kid, I wanted to be a vet and then I realized I wasn't really a science or math person. This business is the next best thing, if not better. Here it's all about fun. Everyone that comes to Camp Bow Wow is happy to be here. The dogs are happy to be here. The customers are happy to be here. The reality of being a vet is that there is a sad part to it, but here it's all fun.

Q. Did you work on your own to find your franchise or did you work with someone? If so, who and tell me about that process.

A. We just worked with the couple that we ultimately bought our first franchise with, whom we later sold our first territory to.

Q. What was your biggest fear in deciding to purchase your franchise?

A. I think the biggest fear was probably what most people would have, which is, "what if it fails?" I had always wanted to go the entrepreneurial route and my wife is a CPA, so we are complete opposites. She lives in the world of black and white. She sees businesses fail, but I live in the more entrepreneurial dreamer realm. That fear was never realized. Our first location in Colorado Springs was extremely successful and is still one of the most successful camps in the franchise system and Fort Collins is great too. I love it. It's made me happy.

> "People can go to any town and they look for a name they recognize and trust..."

Q. What was the best and worst advice you received while you were investigating your franchise purchase?

A. For me, the difficulty was the fact that my friends and family are from South Dakota and their mindset of the way you treat a dog is very different than here in Colorado. A dog in

South Dakota is more like the dog that you put in the background. My family and friends thought I was crazy. They absolutely thought I was throwing my money down the toilet. I felt there were people out there that were just like me. People who don't want to stick their dog in a cage for almost 24 hours a day when they travel or are out of the house. When people send their dog to a typical boarding business, the dog gets let out for a walk a couple times a day. Other then that, the dogs are stuck in a cage. I hated that concept. I never boarded my dogs. I would send them off to my friend's house.

In terms of good advice, I do want to add that my dad was always very encouraging of going the franchising route. We have had a family business for over 100 years, but he knew that in the franchise business I was going to get a game plan to help me get ahead.

Q. How did you go about funding your franchise when you bought it?
A. We borrowed money from my wife's parents.

Q. What was the biggest challenge you have had in building your business? Did you anticipate this challenge? How have you overcome it?
A. I think the biggest challenge is realizing that you are going to be wearing a lot of hats starting up your own business. You are running the front desk and taking care of the dogs out back. If your computer breaks down, you've got to fix the computer. If the drains get plugged, you've got to figure out how to fix that too. You have to have answers to every single issue affecting your business. I didn't quite anticipate that, but now five years later, it's a lot easier. You realize you have to rely on people to succeed. I cannot do everything.

> "...he knew that in the franchise business I was going to get a game plan to help me get ahead."

I can't be out back watching the dogs, and taking care of the customers, and fixing the computers, and making sure the tubs are clean. I need to rely on others to help me. I am a big believer in working hard, but I could never work 100 hours a week. I knew that I would be a failure if I did that, so I started saying, "Okay, I have to completely trust my employees." I think that was my biggest challenge.

Q. Where do you see yourself and your business five years from now?
A. Hopefully we will add another location or even more. I'd like to own a territory big enough to sustain that and I think as long as we keep plugging along we will get there.

Q. Are you having fun? Are you making money? Would you do it again?
A. I'd have to say "Yes" to all three. We are making money and we are having a lot of fun.

"Desire is the key to motivation, but it's determination and commitment to an unrelenting pursuit of your goal - a commitment to excellence - that will enable you to attain the success you seek."
                                    -Mario Andretti

2

Troy Cook, CertaPro Painters and Shelf Genie

BACKGROUND
Before launching his successful career as a franchise owner, Troy Cook worked on over 80 feature films. He began writing and directing his first film at age 24. Troy was a child actor. He was also an assistant manager at *McDonalds*. A black cat with no tail named Ranger, rules over his house in Colorado.

INTERVIEW
Q. What franchise did you purchase and when?
A. I purchased *CertaPro Painters* franchise about 12 years ago. I have since sold that franchise. I bought a *Shelf Genie* franchise two years ago.

Q. When was *CertaPro Painters* founded and how many existing franchisees are there in their system?
A. *CertaPro Painters* was founded about five years before I bought it. It's close to 20 years old now. It was fairly robust at the time I purchased it, they already had a couple hundred franchisees in their system.

Q. What were you doing for work prior to opening your initial franchise?

A. I was a film director. I started off as a camera man and worked for about 14 years in that industry, working my way up through the ranks to writing and directing movies and commercials.

Q. Had you ever run a business before opening your franchise? If not, how was that transition like?

A. I think you can draw from all your work experience in helping you run a business. From the directing standpoint, I was already used to working really long hours. Our minimum work week was about 72 hours. If you are running your own business, I think it's wise to plan on that many hours to get things off the ground. I also learned how to manage lots of people. When you are directing a movie, you might have 150 people underneath you. You are all working together to make something happen. I drew from that experience for managing painters in my painting company.

Q. What attracted you to the franchise concept as opposed to starting up a business on your own?

A. The statistics that I learned from speaking with franchise brokers. Franchise businesses, at their five year point of operation, are 80% more likely to be in business versus if they started their own business from scratch. That was very compelling to me. Also, the idea that franchises have a system that's been proven through trial and error, and work well in a lot of different parts of the country, highly interested me.

> *"I think you can draw from all your work experience in helping you run a business."*

Q. Which other franchises did you consider in your search?

A. One business that was a finalist for me was an oil change type company. It was very successful. The guys I talked to who were running it seemed very knowledgeable, and made plenty of money. The start-up costs were about five or six times more then that of the company I ended up purchasing. In the end, I don't think I could have made more money for that extra cost.

Q. Did you work on your own to find your franchise or did you work with someone?

A. When I bought *CertaPro Painters* I worked on my own. When I bought *Shelf Genie*, I did use a franchise consultant. I told him, "I am looking for this kind of business that does such-and-such-and-such. Please narrow it down for me so I don't have to look through everything." He did that, but he also conducted some personality assessments which factored into the recommendations he came up with during his investigations.

Q. What was your biggest fear in deciding to purchase your franchise and how did you get over it? Was this fear ever realized?

A. My biggest fear for buying any business at all, was making a mistake in purchasing a company that I would have trouble running, or that it ended up not being a good monetary investment. When I bought my first business, I was in the process of moving to Colorado where my wife's family lives. I was moving away from a business where I was used to making a six figure income. That made me very nervous. Those fears drove me to work really hard and to make sure that I did the best decision making I could. I did a lot of research. I did drive-alongs with multiple franchisees before I considered buying the company. As a result, I learned a lot about how to be successful and how to avoid mistakes. In the end, by talking to enough franchisees and doing a fair amount of due

> *"Franchise businesses, at their five year point of operation, are 80% more likely to be in business versus if they started their own business from scratch."*

diligence, I was able to find out enough specifics about what was positive and negative about the company. My investigation turned out to be right on the money.

Q. What was the best and worst advice you received while you were investigating your franchise purchase?
A. I am fairly independent. I relied on my own instincts and on my investigation. I did not receive any good or bad advice that impacted my decision to move forward.

Q. Do you feel that you have received adequate support from your franchise parent in growing your business? What are some areas for improvement, if any?
A. *CertaPro Painters* and *Shelf Genie* are both well run companies. *CertaPro Painters*, in particular, definitely had their processes down. They definitely had all the support you would ever need. At their national conventions, the advice of the franchisees was invaluable. We received excellent training as well. For *Shelf Genie*, being that it's newer, there aren't quite as many franchisees. That being said, the support within the company promotes the same idea of sharing among the network. Those things are really helpful.

> *"I did drive-alongs with multiple franchisees before I considered buying the company."*

Q. How did you go about funding your franchise?
A. My initial purchase, *CertaPro Painters*, didn't require a huge amount of money since it was a service business. I used personal savings. I opened up a couple different credit cards to assist with cash flow. That was it. For *Shelf Genie*, because I had success with *CertaPro Painters*, it was a lot easier to find traditional business financing.

Q. What was the biggest challenge you had in building your business? Did you anticipate this challenge and how did you overcome it?

A. The biggest challenge was always finding enough quality employees for *CertaPro Painters*. It was a lot of trial and error. That was absolutely, hands down, the hardest challenge to growing. I could have grown faster if I could have found more quality employees. I grew about 50% each year for the first few years, and I started off fairly huge to begin with. It all worked out in the end.

With *Shelf Genie*, the challenge is that business is often impacted by the economy. It's often a need versus want item. I am still working on how to get past this hurdle. The other challenges are not having quite the same advertising resources as they have nationwide. I'm not always able to take advantage of the resources available in the larger markets.

Q. Where do you see yourself and your business five years from now?

A. Five years from now I expect to be well known within my business area, so my advertising will have reached everyone by that point. To be honest, I believe that five years is a good time for selling a franchise. I will probably be thinking about selling that one and moving on and starting a new franchise.

Q. Are you having fun, are you making money, and would you do it again?

A. I am mostly having fun. There are days that are difficult. *Shelf Genie* is a fun franchise. I do some of the installations on it and some of the sales. I do a little bit of everything. I enjoy it. It's a lot smaller scale of a company, so there is less stress that way, which I appreciate. I am making money and I would do it again. *CertaPro Painters*, on a day-to-day basis, was not as much fun because there's a lot more stress involved in having that many painters working for you, but you make a very large amount of money doing it. If you can handle that many painters and the stress, it's a great franchise.

Q. Do you have any other parting thoughts on your experience in franchising? Would you recommend franchising for people who are contemplating jumping out of a corporate career, or thinking about starting their business as a viable opportunity?

A. I am a huge fan of franchising so yes, I do recommend it. I don't think I could have ever of started a painting company on my own, or any other company for that matter, and have grown it to be as large as it was. It was earning millions of dollars worth of business in such a short time. I couldn't have gotten to that place without the help and guidance of the franchise system. That being said, you still have to do your research on the franchise you purchase.

3

Betty Corbitt, Gotcha Covered

BACKGROUND

Betty Corbitt is the owner/operator of Gotcha Covered, a custom window coverings franchise. "After 30 plus years working in the retail industry, I had faith that there was a business opportunity that would allow me to control my schedule and income. Stephen Hogan, a representative from FranChoice, and a former SCORE volunteer, guided me in finding such a business endeavor," Betty Corbitt recounts.

INTERVIEW

Q. What franchise did you purchase and when?

A. The franchise that I purchased was originally called *V2K Window Décor and More*. I purchased it November of 2008. Since then, *V2K* has merged with another window treatment franchise called *Gotcha Covered*. Because of the catchiness of the name, all of the franchises were given the opportunity to re-brand, which is what I did at the first of this year.

Q. When was this company founded and how many franchises are there in the system?

A. The people who founded *V2K*, had been in the window covering business in some way, shape, or form since the late 50's, but they actually started franchising in 2001. At the present time there are approximately 130 active franchisees across the United Sates, Canada, and Aruba.

Q. What were you doing for work prior to opening your franchise?
A. Before I purchased my franchise, I had a long history working in retail. I had 24 years collectively with Macy's and the BonMarce/Macy's organization.

Q. Had you ever run a business before opening your franchise?
A. I had a business prior to this business. In 1987, my husband was working in an industry that provided an opportunity for me to own a surface company, so I jumped on that chance. I started a service business which we operated for four years prior to my husband's passing from cancer. After that, I returned to retail work. My son was two at the time and being the sole-surviving parent, I took the safe route with the benefits. Because of my expertise, I felt confident that I could get a job and I did so quickly. I was employed as a department sales manager and a group sales manager for Macy's. I then held a position as an assistant manager for a woman's specialty clothing store. During all that time, I yearned for the opportunity to control my own schedule. I wanted to be involved in the community and to duplicate the income that I was making as a retail manager.

Q. What attracted you to the franchise concept as opposed to starting up a business on your own?
A. I did consider starting up a business on my own. Because of my extensive experience in retail I thought, "How could I do things differently? What type of product would be attractive in this community?" I had considered the financial outlay and the

> *"...I crossed paths with a franchise consultant who gave me some very attractive options."*

thought of being locked to a brick and mortar store. As I was going through the due diligence part of my investigation and learning various issues of starting up my own business, it was fortuitous that I crossed paths with a franchise consultant who gave me some very attractive options.

Q. Did you consider other franchises in your search? If so, which ones?
A. The three presented to me were of course *V2K*, a home health care/respite business, and an art enrichment program that was affiliated with *Crayola Crayons*.

Q. What attracted you to the franchise you now run and how did you determine this was the best franchise for you?
A. It was definitely through a process of elimination. I had calls with other franchise owners and each of the franchise corporate offices. The more questions I asked, the more answers I got, and the more analyzing I did. *V2K* really rose to the top because it capitalized on my previous experience, my creativity and my passion for networking and marketing. It seemed to fill a niche in the Southeastern Washington area with the economic downturn and the fact that building construction was still going strong, both commercially and residentially. I saw that there still was a need for window coverings.

Q. Did you work on your own to find your franchise or did you work with someone?
A. I became acquainted with a franchise consultant. At the time, I was still in the process of almost signing a lease on my own business. I happened to be introduced to this franchise consultant through a seminar he was doing on franchises. I signed up for the meeting and I was the only attendee. I got a one-on-one experience with Stephen Hogan, who works for *FranChoice*. He was also, for many years, a volunteer for SCORE. Instead of telling me what I should do, he gave me options and talked about the pros and cons so that I could make my own decision. At first I had not considered a fran-

chise, but the more in depth I got with my due diligence, the more attractive the option looked to me.

Q. What was your biggest fear in deciding to purchase your franchise? How did you get over it and was this fear ever realized?

A. My biggest fear, which most people experience in this process, was the fear of failure. It was fleeting, however. It wasn't overpowering. My other concern was getting the business started. I was concerned about all of the things I had to do in order to get established in the community as a business. Between the licensing, the contractor's registration, the networking, I worried about all the steps I had to take in order to become a viable business. I realized it was going to be very labor and time intensive.

I have been actively engaged in this business for a year and a half. The level of business activity that I am experiencing at this point in time, has probably more than doubled from the activity that I had last year. I have been given, through my association with Stephen Hogan, the skills to develop some foresight into imagining how I want my business to look like next year and five years after that.

> *"At first I had not considered a franchise, but the more in depth I got with my due diligence, the more attractive the option looked to me."*

In February, after exhibiting at a home and garden show, I realized a great response to my business and the need for people who had challenging windows. There were builders that were building homes, and people buying homes, so there really was a need for my service in the community. This year I am definitely taking steps to envision how I want my business to look like next year. I have hired sales consultants. I have an office assistant. I have a very proficient installer and it is still very exciting to see where my business is taking me.

Q. Do you feel you have received adequate support from your franchise parent in growing your business? What are some areas for improvement, if any?
A. I had the great fortune of having an advisor with *V2K*, who was the franchise development director, work with me. We spoke weekly during what they call their *90-day quick start* program. He was awesome about offering suggestions and being supportive and helped with problem solving. This was great. However, he did not have all the specifics of how to operate in certain states, which sometimes can be an issue. I think that if *Gotcha Covered* is going to promote *Gotcha Covered* across the United States, they need to be a little bit more aware of all the various state requirements for doing business.

Q. How did you go about funding your franchise purchase?
A. Through my relationship with Stephen Hogan, I was directed to some companies that help people buy businesses and fund them. I funded my business through one of those businesses, *Fran Fund*, which enables a person to take advantage of certain IRS loop holes. I formed a corporation and converted my IRA into a self-administered 401K, which I then used to buy my franchise and fund my initial start-up costs.

Q. What was the biggest challenge you had in building your business and did you anticipate this challenge? How have you overcome it?
A. The biggest challenge for me was all of the steps I had to take to get the business up and running and trying out different marketing venues just to see which worked and which didn't work. Being a self-employed person I have always considered myself to be disciplined, but you really have to be very self-disciplined in managing your time. You are the one who is wholly responsible for your income. I was putting in 14 hours a day, seven days a week on just learning about the

product, learning about how to design a window treatment, and how to work our company's exclusive design software. I believe I'm now overcoming all of those challenges.

Q. Where do you see yourself and your business five years from now?

A. That's a good question because I am still formulating that in my mind. One of the recommended books that Stephen Hogan had suggested I read, *The E-myth Revisited*, talked about not being burdened by every single aspect of my business, so that I could do the things that I do best. This is why I hired an office assistant. I knew there were some very important tasks that were integral to marketing and I realized I needed some help in doing those things. Five years from now, I see myself potentially having a small show room and having more design consultants. I want to be the go-to person for custom window coverings. There are so many more products that are available in my franchise, like decorative home and office accessories. I am always looking for other opportunities for gaps in the market that would be beneficial to add to my product line.

> *"I formed a corporation and converted my IRA into a self-administered 401K, which I then used to buy my franchise and fund my initial start-up costs."*

Q. Are you having fun? Are you making money? Would you do it again?

A. Yes, I am having fun. It's kind of grown to a different level now, but I really enjoy what I am doing. Am I making money? Yes. As of last month, I am now paying myself a salary. I had enough money saved up and enough resources to go almost 18 months of supporting myself without having to draw money off the business. I pay my office assistant an hourly wage. Would I do it again? Yes, absolutely.

Q. Do you have any other parting comments or words of wisdom?

A. I have so much faith in entrepreneurship and with the spirit of the American people. I think often times our economy is affected by news, whether that bad news is valid or not. We have become so dependent on hearing and making decisions based not only on our own experience, but on what other people say. Optimism is on the rise and I think that if anyone were to put their mind to doing something where they truly believe in their ability, then they will be successful.

"Faith is taking the first step even when you don't see the whole staircase."
                                               -Martin Luther King, Jr.

WAYPOINT

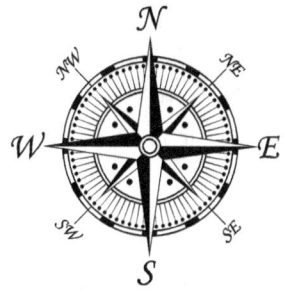

Don't Waste Your Time

During your franchise research, how can you quickly identify those franchise companies that aren't right for you?

If you've done any research on franchise opportunities, you've surely discovered that there is an overwhelming number of franchised businesses available. According to an article in Franchising World magazine, by 2006, franchising in the U.S. had expanded to more than 3,000 franchise concepts in over 230 industry sectors. For someone interested in purchasing a franchise, that's a lot of ground to cover!

What you need are some simple tests to apply in your research so you can quickly eliminate those companies that aren't a fit for you. By simplifying the initial research process, you'll have more time (and enthusiasm!) for those companies that may be potential winners.

Here are the A, B, Cs of franchise research:

A. Your Goals. The most important step is to set your goals for franchise ownership. After all, if you don't know where you're going, how will you know when you've arrived? Ask yourself what sort of characteristics you'd like your business to have. Do you want to manage many employees or just a few? Are you passionate about B2B sales or would you prefer a retail location where customers come to you? Do you intend to keep your current job while the business starts or do you want to be a hands-on business owner? Carefully consider all you expect from business ownership and make a list of these goals. They will help you quickly determine if any franchise you look at is worth the time to complete a thorough investigation.

Once you have determined your goals, there are a few other key tests that you can quickly use to make sure you're looking at a franchise that might be a good match for you. You'll need to contact the franchisor and ask to see their Franchise Disclosure Document (FDD) to complete the next series of tests.

B. **Investment Requirements.** Examine the amount of net worth and liquidity that is required by the franchise. There's no sense spending lots of time investigating a franchise that you can't afford. While there may be some leeway in these numbers, no good franchisor will want a franchisee to start a business deeply in debt so consider these numbers and eliminate any company that requires more than you can manage.

C. **Territory Limitations.** Ask the franchisor if there are viable territory options available within the area that you are interested in locating a business. If not, move on.

D. **Litigation.** Item 3 in the FDD requires the franchisor to disclose all relevant litigation history. Reviewing and questioning the information in this section can allow you to quickly form an opinion about the relationship values of the franchisor. If there are a number of unhappy former franchisees, you can pretty well assume the franchisor has some problems to fix before you would consider the business for yourself.

E. **Failure Rates.** Item 20 in the FDD requires the franchisor to disclose all relevant data concerning unit failures and turnover rates at specific locations. If the track record doesn't look strong enough to you, there is no reason to proceed.

F. Required Skill Sets. If you get past the factors listed above, ask the franchisor to give you a list of the characteristics and skills they consider essential for a franchisee to be successful in their system. If these don't match your skills or if they are inconsistent with your goals for a business, head for the door.

Once you have made it past these first six steps with one or more businesses, you can dig more deeply into each franchise. Don't even consider skipping this next step because it is the most important test your new business will have to "pass" before you can be sure you know everything possible about a potential franchise purchase.

G. Existing Franchisees. Get on the phone and call a number of the existing franchisees; you'll find their contact information in the FDD. Find out how they feel about their businesses and also about the support they've received from the franchisor. Spend the time it takes to get a sense of the system from their perspective. Keep a record of their responses to your questions. If you find an overwhelming consistency in their input, it is a great indicator of how you would end up feeling if you become a franchisee in this system.

There! You've put your list of potential franchise companies through six quick tests and one much longer but extremely important test. If you've found some franchise businesses that made it through this testing process, you can be sure that they are likely to have the right stuff to make you a happy and successful franchisee. What's left? Talk to the franchisor's development people, make a visit to their corporate headquarters, and then ...ta da ... make your decision!

"Knowing others is intelligence; knowing yourself is true wisdom. Mastering others is strength; mastering yourself is true power."

- Lao Tzu

4

Sarah Kruse, Seeking Sitters

BACKGROUND

Sarah Kruse is the owner of six *Seeking Sitters* locations throughout Colorado's front range. As the mom of three active boys, Sarah knows firsthand how hard it can be to find a trustworthy and reliable babysitter. Balancing her career and family life has been a motivating factor for Sarah to become a business owner. *Seeking Sitters* gives Sarah the flexibility to maintain her professional career and still be able to be there for her family.

Sarah has her MA in counseling psychology and was a high school counselor for seven years before owning her own business. She volunteers her time with the her children's schools, the *Junior League of Fort Collins*, as a board member for the *Child Advocacy Center* and is on the steering committee for *Leadership Fort Collins*.

INTERVIEW

Q. What franchise did you purchase and when?

A. We purchased *Seeking Sitters*. It was almost four years ago that we purchased Fort Collins and Boulder, Colorado. Then we purchased North Denver, Central Denver, and South Denver. Six months ago we purchased Douglas County.

Q. When was this company founded and how many existing franchisees are there in the system?
A. It was founded in 2004. I believe there are 51 franchisees.

Q. Had you ever run a business before being a high school counselor? What was the transition like?
A. I had not run a business prior to this and it was kind of like going into shock at first because we were so busy so quickly. I really do like the flexibility that *Seeking Sitters* has given our family and the ability for me to be with our kids whenever I need to be. I really, really appreciate that fact. The hardest part is I don't have any time to myself anymore. My phone rings non-stop 24 hours a day and because of the nature of our business I don't really get a break.

Q. What attracted you to the franchise concept as opposed to starting up the business on your own?
A. With my master's degree in counseling, I wasn't really prepared for running a business. At least not for all the business aspects involved. My husband has his MBA, so I wanted to have our first business to be something where we did not have to reinvent the wheel and we could just step into it. We wanted something turn-key. We could gradually step into the business rather than having to start from ground zero.

Q. Did you consider other franchises in your search? If so, which ones?
A. We did. We actually looked at starting a kid's culinary studio. That was actually what I was really excited about. My husband however, convinced me that was not going to be a very good move since the start-up was enormous and I would be babysitting other people's kids and cleaning up after them, which is something I had no desire to

> *"I wanted to have our first business to be something where we did not have to re-invent the wheel and we could just step into it."*

do. We found the babysitting business, *Seeking Sitters*, and initially it was not something I was very excited about, but my husband was really gung-ho about it.

Q. What attracted you to the franchise you now run and how did you determine this was the best franchise for you?

A. The first consideration was that we had three kids that were all young at the time. We had personally experienced the hardship of trying to find a great babysitter; somebody which we felt comfortable leaving three active boys with. The start-up costs were reasonable as well. We did not have to have a store front; you could run it from your home. The business seemed so well put together. It seemed like they had thought of everything. When we actually met David and Adrian Cartwright, who are the franchisors, we found them to be amazing! They helped us every step of the way, at the beginning. We were the fourth location and the first location that they didn't know previously. We got in very early and had the benefit of having their undivided attention.

Q. Did you work on your own to find your franchise or did you work with someone?

A. We worked on our own.

Q. What was your biggest fear in deciding to purchase your franchise? How did you get over it and was this fear ever realized?

A. I think the biggest fear was wondering if we would be sucked into something where we would not make any money. Also, we wondered if the franchisors were going to tell you what to do in every step of our business. Thankfully, that was not even remotely what we got into.

> *"We got in very early and had the benefit of having their undivided attention."*

Q. What was the best advice you received while you were investigating your franchise purchase?
A. The good advice was we should get our attorney to look over all the documents and make sure they were favorable for us and not just for the franchise system. We also met with our accountant.

Q. Do you feel like you have received adequate support from your franchise parent in growing your business? What are some areas of improvement, if any?
A. Absolutely. I think that we received amazing attention. I think for the first six months, I was on the phone with Adrian Cartwright at least once a day! She literally held my hand as we got started which was so nice and so helpful. One of the other benefits to working with *Seeking Sitters* is that they have such a great group of franchisees. For the newer franchisees that are coming in, they are put in contact with other franchisees that have been in business a bit longer than they have. So if they have any questions they have someone to contact. They've created a support network within the franchise system which is really nice.

Q. How did you go about funding your franchise?
A. We did it in three stages. In the first phase we took out a second mortgage on our house. We followed up with a traditional small business loan.

Q. What was the biggest challenge you have had in building your business?
A. I think there are some times when marketing really works, and sometimes it can work too well. In the business we have, it's all about balance between the number of members that we have, the number of sitters that we have, and the number of requests that come in. There are sometimes when all of a sudden those numbers get thrown out of balance and you feel like the ground has been pulled out from beneath you. When you are growing too quickly, it can become not so

good. People laugh when I say that, but you have to grow at a moderate rate where you can keep up with the demand; people can be disappointed. Balance in general, is the biggest challenge for any business owner. Striking a balance between work and family can be tough in the beginning. I really do think about balance and knowing where your limits are, and what is healthy and what's not.

Q. Where do you see yourself and your business five years from now?

A. I don't think that we will still be doing *Seeking Sitters* in five years. My kids have gotten to the age where they are growing out of a need to have a babysitter and the oldest is going to be the babysitter of our family. So for us, relevancy is going to kind of outgrow the need for the *Seeking Sitters* franchise. We signed a five-year agreement. We might do one more round, but I see this as a catapult into us starting our own business, not necessarily as a franchisee, but as an independent business owner.

Q. Are you having fun, are you making money, and would you do it again?

A. Yes, yes, and yes!

"Our calling is the point at which our deepest gladness meets the world's deepest need."

- Frederick Buechner

Jim Lautzenheiser, Big O Tires and Grease Monkey

BACKGROUND

Jim holds a BSBA from the Ohio State University. Before purchasing his own *Big O Tires* franchise in 1996, he worked for *Big O Tires* Corporate headquarters as their Regional Credit Manager and Regional Sales Manager. He lives in Fort Collins, Colorado.

INTERVIEW

Q. What franchise did you purchase and when?

A. We purchased our first franchise, *Big O Tires*, in December of 1996. That was our first venture. We had that for about four years and then we decided to open up our second franchise, *Grease Monkey*, on September 17, 2001.

Q. When were these companies founded and how many existing franchisees are there in the system?

A. Big O has 550 stores and Grease Monkey about 260.

Q. What were you doing prior to you opening the franchise?

A. I worked for *Good Year Tire and Rotor Company*. I was their district sales manager in Southern California.

Q. Had you ever run a business before opening the franchise?
A. Never. There was a huge, huge learning curve. Going from never really managing a staff before, to managing an automotive staff was huge. You have to deal with the different personalities of the staff and focus on the quality of the people that you have to hire. It is difficult when you are used to working for a corporation where everyone is responsible. Going into an industry where people have a hard time showing up on time, tucking their shirt in, and shaving, was initially pretty difficult.

Q. What attracted you to the franchise concept as opposed to starting up a business on your own?
A. My father worked for *Big O* corporate for 15 years prior to us opening our store and he had opened 200 stores himself on the franchisor side. That was pretty compelling. We had a real strong foot hold in *Big O* and that made a real easy transition going from corporate to this.

Q. Did you consider other franchises in your search?
A. Because of my existing experience with *Big O Tire*, this was the only business I considered. I had all the numbers and the experience from my father's role at the company, so it was just a matter of executing it.

Q. What attracted you to the franchises you now run and how did you determine this was the best franchise for you?
A. For *Big O*, if you wanted to get into the tire business, they were the largest independent franchise organization in the country. I assumed they would have the best marketing available. Purchasing power is everything in the tire business because it's a commodity, so if you are not the lowest price, or very close to the lowest price, it is hard to compete in that market. You have to align yourself with a large buyer.

Q. Did you work on your own, or with someone, to find your franchise?
A. I didn't work with anybody. My dad was involved in the busi-

ness already.

Q. What was your biggest fear in deciding to purchase a franchise and how did you get over it? Was this fear ever realized?

A. I was so naïve. Sometimes ignorance is great! When you are just starting you don't really know all the risks. Our motto was, "Failure is not an option." Basically, I did whatever it was going to take to be successful. I worked the store six days a week for five years from open to close, because I couldn't initially afford having employees on payroll. A lot of people can't maintain that after the first year. They don't want to work that hard and they give up. They just burn themselves out. Cash flow was the biggest hurdle the first year. People should never go in under-capitalized into this business. Always go in over capitalized. Don't go in with borrowed capital out of your home equity. SBA loans and other business financing are fine, but you don't want to go in with credit card debt to open your business. Once you go negative, it's hard to find another source of money to keep funding your business.

Q. How did you go about funding the franchise?

A. I got an SBA loan. We were also concerned about owning the real estate where our business was located. That's the game plan you want to play in small business. Let the business pay for the building and the land for yourself. That is our exit strategy. The day you begin your business is the day you try to plan to get out of your business. Our exit strategy was to own the real estate.

> *"Our motto was, 'Failure is not an option.' Basically, I did whatever it was going to take to be successful."*

Q. What was the best advice you received while investigating your purchase?

A. Because of how I got into the business, through my father's connection, all of the investigation and consideration was all done before I even got involved.

Q. Do you feel you have received adequate support from the franchise parent in growing your business? What are some areas, if any, for improvement?

A. The most important thing is don't rely on the franchise to make you successful. Everybody wants to blame the franchisor on their failure if they close up their business, but it wasn't just the franchisor's fault. If you are going to rely on the franchisor to make you successful, you will fail. Forget about the franchisor; they are there to help you, but they are not there to make you successful. You have to make your business successful. You have to go out into the community. You have to work the store. You have to do the marketing and advertising and so forth. Just rely on the franchisor as support for you, not to make you successful.

> *"Purchasing power is everything...you have to align yourself with a large buyer."*

Q. What was the biggest challenge you have had in building your business? Did you anticipate this challenge? How have you overcome it?

A. The biggest challenge was realizing that when the economy takes a hit, not every franchise model is going to work for every market. I learned this when we opened our Windsor, Colorado *Grease Monkey*. The text book model that came from *Grease Monkey* wasn't working anymore. For 15 years I executed the *Big O* model and then we went out and opened the *Grease Monkey*, which had their own systems. We quickly realized there wasn't enough business to make their model work for us. We had to look at adding additional services. We added tires and a mechanic in our *Grease Monkey* store. We had to think outside the box.

Q. Where do you see yourself and your business five years from now?

A. Five years from now I want to develop the internal people and the managers I have right now, with the hopes of getting them on as partners. That way, I can start my exit strategy 10 to 15 years from now. The best way a small business can exit in today's environment, is not typically through a third-party buyer. Our strategy is to develop our employees into partners and let them have a buy-in into the business. Our employee now is a part-owner of the business.

Q. Are you having fun and are you making money? If you had to do it all over again, would you?

A. Yes, I am having fun today. In the 15 years I have been doing this, I would say around years four and five, I thought differently. At that time I felt I was paying money to be at my business everyday, and was working 80 hour work weeks. I thought, "What is the point of this all?" If you can make it through that point, and as your business grows and develops and your sales exceed your overhead, then it was well worth the effort. Now I am sitting here 15 years later with my buildings being paid off within the next six years. I am 40 years old, and I could be retired in eight or nine years. By age 50, I could be financially comfortable.

"Man cannot discover new oceans unless he has the courage to lose sight of the shore."

- Lord Chesterfield

WAYPOINT

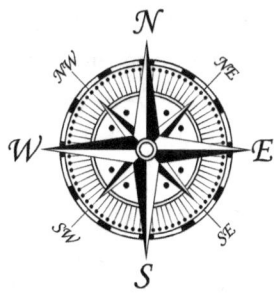

Employer or Employee?

WHERE DO YOU FIT – ARE YOU CUT OUT TO BE AN EMPLOYER OR AN EMPLOYEE?

Have you ever wondered why some people own a business and others just work for one? Maybe you've thought about owning a business of your own for some time but you're not sure if it's the right step to take.

What kind of an individual is cut out to be an EMPLOYER? Usually it is someone who sees an opportunity and has the commitment and courage to go for what he wants. That opportunity may come with obstacles, but the employer will see around the obstacles to his goal. He knows there will be challenges and even welcomes them. Why? Because he or she loves a challenge and knows that the difficulties in life separate the doers from the dreamers, the EMPLOYERS from the EMPLOYEES.

An employer is not someone who shies away from hard work. He is willing to put in whatever time is necessary to create his ideal opportunity. But the hard work always has a carrot dangling at the end in the form of success. With this success comes financial security and personal flexibility. An employer understands that over time, as he becomes more comfortable with employees assuming more of the daily operations, he will be able to step away from the business to some degree while having a valuable asset working for him.

Someone cut out to be an employer has envisioned the end

results from the beginning and worked tirelessly toward establishing that result. Challenges are met, problems are smoothed over and eventually the employees provide the employer with a nice and comfortable living.

Finally, someone with an EMPLOYER personality has passion. He will put his heart into a project and truly believes not only in what he's doing but also in his ability to obtain the desired results.

What kind of an individual is the EMPLOYEE? An employee is not comfortable with risks and sees challenges not as opportunities but as insurmountable obstacles. He has thought about business ownership but lacks the desire to step outside of his comfort zone. Comfort is foremost on his list of desirable job qualities and he would find working long hours while establishing a business distasteful.

The employee maintains his status quo and wonders why he's not getting ahead. He punches his timecard every day while the employer makes money from his efforts. He imagines he'd take the step to business ownership if only the right opportunity came along and wonders why the stars have never been perfectly aligned for him to realize his dream. He doesn't understand that the stars don't align themselves and have never been perfectly aligned for anyone, including his employer.

There are lots of examples of people who've overcome obstacles through perseverance. It took Thomas Edison ten years to develop a practical alkaline battery, conducting over 28,000 tests. Further, he didn't let lack of education stop him. He had three months of formal education and after that was home-schooled by his mother. But he had a passion for invention and believed in himself.

Prior to creating Mickey Mouse, Walt Disney created Oswald the Lucky Rabbit. He managed to sell the cartoons through a distributor only to find that the distributor had gone behind his back and signed up most of his animators, hoping to make the Oswald cartoons in his own studio for less money. Disney also lost the rights to the character he created – talk about major career obstacles! Of course you know this part of the story: Disney went on to create a new character, a loveable mouse whose name has been a household word for half a century. As for Oswald the Lucky Rabbit – Oswald who?

Ray Kroc was just a milk shake maker salesman when he discovered a hamburger stand in California that was using eight of his mixers at a time. When he visited the restaurant he was amazed to see so many customers served so quickly. He convinced the restaurant owners, Dick and Mac McDonald, to open more of their restaurants and then proposed he be the one to manage them. Today McDonald's has more than 30,000 McDonald's restaurants in 119 countries and adds about 100 franchisees a year. Ray may not have envisioned everything that McDonald's has become but he was able to see the value of a quick service restaurant to the public and is often credited with making the franchise model an America staple.

What about you? Where do you fit? Are you content to let life happen around you or do you want to be the person making things happen? Business owners see beyond the barriers of entry into business and focus on the carrot dangling at the end of the stick. Employees dwell on the barriers.

If you are ready to make a transition from employee to employer, becoming a franchisee is a great vehicle. The franchisor provides the business model and the training, the brand and the operating system. You provide some capital, a lot of hard work and your passion. Without visionaries there would be no alkaline battery or Disney World or Big Mac. If being a business owner is your dream, believe in yourself and go for it!

"The law of work does seem utterly unfair - but there it is, and nothing can change it; the higher the pay in enjoyment the worker gets out of it, the higher shall be his pay in money also."

— Mark Twain

6

Stephen Lautzenhiser, PuroClean

BACKGROUND
Stephen is the owner and General Manager of *PuroClean Restoration Services* in Fort Collins, Colorado. He previously worked in high tech in business development in California. He holds an MSEE from Stanford and a MS in management from MIT Sloan. He enjoys fly fishing, gardening, and spending time with his wife and two children.

INTERVIEW
Q. What franchise did you purchase and when?
A. We purchased a *PuroClean* franchise in September of 2005.

Q. When was this company founded and how many existing franchisees are there in the system?
A. It was founded in 1990 and there are over 300 active franchisees in our network across the U.S.

Q. What were you doing for work prior to you opening the franchise?
A. I was in business development and sales with *Cisco Systems* and in the semiconductor industry in the Bay Area/Silicon

Valley area of California. I was very much in a white collar type of position before switching over to something this hands on.

Q. Had you ever run a business before opening your franchise?
A. I only had corporate positions before taking on this venture. I guess the opportunity was to really get hands on and embrace all aspects. It turns out you work harder when it's your own sweat equity.

Q. What attracted you to the franchise concept as opposed to starting up a business on your own?
A. Many businesses, especially those that are retail focused, don't have a great success rate. Franchises provide a business formula and structure that can help you get over the hurdle of starting up. We were looking for one that had a return without an inordinately large capital investment.

Q. Did you consider other franchises in your search? If so, which ones?
A. We worked with a franchise consultant and we narrowed it down to five business opportunities. One was called *Pop-A-Lock*, which is a service that helps you get in your house or car if you are locked out. There were a couple that were more retail-oriented that, even though the investment level was within our range, we ruled them out because the business model just didn't fit us.

> *"Franchises provide a business formula and structure that can help you get over the hurdle of starting up."*

Q. What attracted you to the franchise you now run and how did you determine that this was the best franchise for you?
A. I liked the fact that *PuroClean's* opportunity was both the business to business aspect, and there was interaction with insurance agents and adjusters. The corporate experience I

had and the ability to speak in front of groups and share expertise and develop an industry, that translated there. The part that was new and refreshing and different for me was the empathy factor in working with individual clients at a time when they are in the most need.

Q. Did you work on your own to find your franchise?

A. No. We got in touch with an associate from a firm called *FranChoice* named Stephen Hogan. Stephen took us through a fairly methodical process of evaluation, of his thoughts about what type of profile we were, and what type of company we wanted. It really led us down the path of businesses we never would have considered on our own.

Q. What was your biggest fear in deciding to purchase your franchise and how did you get over it?

A. There is always apprehension in going into a new business and I think the first year of our business was the one where we had to do some gut checks. We wondered if we were going to make it. Persistence, gaining a good reputation, and a little bit of luck, enabled us to turn the corner and start getting repeat business from clients. We entered a fairly competitive market place and that was one thing that kind of surprised me a little bit. I don't think we really knew how many other companies engaged in this kind of activity in our area when we were researching the business.

> *"It turns out you work harder when it's your own sweat equity."*

Q. What was the best advice you received while you were investigating your franchise?

A. I think the best advice I probably received was taking the time to understand the economic mode of the business. We were told by our consultant to make sure you get a comfort factor with the margins involved on a per-job basis.

Q. Do you feel you have received adequate support from your franchise parent in growing your business and what are some areas for improvement, if any?
A. The franchise support center helps us with technical issues on equipment. They have implemented a marketing program to try to improve the *PuroClean* brand recognition primarily with insurance and different carriers, more.

Our system has grown to a more critical mass. I feel they haven't been as proactive in supporting existing franchisees in terms of national brand recognition and getting us on the insurance preferred provider lists. This is an area I'd really like the company to put some efforts into over the next year.

Q. How did you go about funding your franchise purchase?
A. We tied the funding of our franchise to an equity sale of a house and relocation from California. We took the majority of the profits from the sale of our house in California, used it towards the initial capital equipment, the franchise fee and operating expenses.

Q. What has been the biggest challenge you have had in building your business?
A. I think the biggest challenge is instilling in our staff the type of service etiquette that I personally have in going to somebody's residence or commercial presence. Being in someone's house, you have to show empathy, you have to show respect for the contents, you have to be very polite and on time. It's an inconvenience to them and we have to constantly remind ourselves that we are helping them through a difficult period and we get praise if we do it right. I am constantly instilling this attitude in our staff. So developing this customer service attitude among my staff and keeping that edge is probably the most important thing to continuing our success.

Q. Where do you see yourself and the business five years from now?

A. Our contract term is for 20 years. I don't believe we are going to be doing this in 20 years. Maybe in the next five years we might find the opportunity to sell our franchise to somebody that has the same vision and qualifications and wants something that's established and can run it, like a general manager. I think in the next five years we probably would be open to moving on, but not in the next year or two. We are going to try to grow our business by at least 50%.

Q. Are you having fun? Are you making money? Would you do it again?

A. Yes, I'm having fun. There is fun in having your own business and I do get satisfaction from a client that earnestly goes out and shakes your hand and says, "Thank you for helping me through this." There's a genuine good feeling factor from that. Am I making money? Certainly, as you grow the challenge is that the top line grows so does the expense line. We started out from our home, as we were advised to do, and now we have a lease on a building that is 2,350 square feet. So we have a commitment on that front, but we have the cash flow to sustain that and our lifestyle. I probably would do it again. I think I might have done a little more research and learned sooner what the dynamic of the competition was and how tight it was for us. The first year was a bit challenging. In terms of where we are versus where we started, we have come a long way.

> "Persistence, gaining a good reputation, and a little bit of luck, enabled us to turn the corner and start getting repeat business from clients."

Q. If your friends were a little disenchanted with their corporate jobs and expressed they would like to do something else, would you recommend a franchise for them?

A. Yes. I am an example of someone who successfully took the leap out of a corporate job. I knew I wanted to have more equity in my life. Working for a corporation wasn't going to give me that long-term equity or the flexibility I now have in my life. If the weather is nice and the fishing looks good, I can fish on the way to and from jobs. I couldn't do that in my corporate job. We have already recommended and had a couple of our friends purchase franchises. In fact, one friend purchased a *PuroClean* business in Southern California!

Sean McEntire, CertaPro Painters

BACKGROUND
Sean dedicated his entire adult career to *Verizon*. He started in a clerical role while studying for his undergraduate degree at *Villanova*. He worked his way up the ranks of management within the company, while completing a master of information science program at *Penn State*. After 18 years, he felt as if he had accomplished what he had set out to do, as he had become an executive leader within the company.

With the recent down-turn of the economy, *Verizon* was forced to lay-off thousands of employees. He decided it was time to take his buyout and look for new challenges. He can easily say that the outcome had a silver lining. In these troubled economic times, he's found the strength to make choices that have put him on a path he would not have chosen otherwise. For that, he is grateful.

INTERVIEW
Q. What franchise did you purchase and when?
A. The franchise I purchased was *CertaPro Painters* in Box County, Pennsylvania. I purchased it in August of 2009.

Q. When was this company founded and how many existing franchisees are there in the system?

A. *CertaPro Painters* was founded back in 1997. There are over 330 franchisees now across the continental United States and in Canada. We do about a little more than 50,000 jobs a year as a combined group.

Q. What were you doing for work prior to opening your franchise?

A. I had spent just about all of my career, the past 19 years, working at *Verizon Communications*. I started when I was in college when I was a freshman. Telco became deregulated and over the years, there have been many mergers and acquisitions. I ultimately left when it became *Verizon*. My last position with the company was as an executive director for *Verizon*, in charge of their billing activities for their large business customers.

Q. Had you ever run a business before? How was the transition from a corporate career to running your own business?

A. I have only been in corporate america. I started when I was a freshman in college. It was a summer job in the mail room that turned into a career. I worked my way up from mail clerk to executive director. Over those years, while at *Verizon*, I wore multiple hats. I was a residential collection rep with a union title. I was a sales manager who had responsibilities for a sales team. I was a center manager who had multiple call centers with hundreds of people reporting to me. I was in staff support position where I was meeting with the executive leadership and setting policy and procedure for different business units. So I had numerous jobs there. I kind of did that purposefully so I could keep my resume well rounded. I have never had my own business.

> *"Franchises give you a model, a process, and then you take your different skills that you have gotten over the years and build upon that."*

What it Takes to Build a Successful Franchise

Q. What attracted you to the franchise concept as opposed to starting up a business on your own?

A. I had no idea how to start my own business and that's one of the things that drove me towards franchises in general. They are a business in a box. Franchises give you a model, a process, and then you take your different skills that you have gotten over the years and build upon that. That's what attracted me to *CertaPro Painters*. I liked their systems support; I liked their scalability model. I thought that I could take my business background in those different fields – operation support, sales support, procedures and policy, management of employees both union and non-union, and put that into this model and be successful.

Q. Did you consider other franchises in your search?

A. One of the things I kind of wanted to do initially was non-medical senior care. I started doing some homework and looking into the business. I discovered that Pennsylvania, where I live, is second behind only Florida in the number of seniors. That's because they have some good pension tax laws here. Everyday more people are eligible for social security in Pennsylvania. I thought it would be a good opportunity. I also was looking at a *Sports Clips* franchise. I also looked into *Rita's Water Ice* franchise in North Carolina. *Rita's* is popular up here; they are not popular or not deployed in the south. I also looked at a cleaning company out of Maryland and finally looked at *CertaPro Painters*, which wasn't on my radar at all.

Q. Did you work on your own to find your franchise or did you work with someone?

A. I worked with Stephen Hogan at *FranChoice*. I found him when I was reading the *Wall Street Journal*. There was an article on *FranChoice* and I went on the internet and Stephen called me. Through the due diligence process, he asked me a number of questions over a couple different interviews he and I had. We talked about my goals, my skill set, what I was looking for, and then he came back to me with a couple different opportunities. It's very funny because I had made it up in my mind that I was going to be selling water ice or taking care of seniors, but here I am selling paint. It wasn't something I was thinking about. He really didn't steer me in any direction, which I was very impressed with and I liked. He said, "Look, I am not going to tell you which one is better. I will give you information on all of them. I will tell you how you need to communicate with them. I will tell you some things you need to do as a potential business owner, but you will have to make the decision and live with it."

Q. What was your biggest fear in deciding to purchase your franchise? How did you get over it and was this fear ever realized?

A. My biggest fear was financial. I had nightmares and heart palpitations about the financial aspects of it. Having spent 19 years at Verizon, I was compensated extremely well. I had a nice salary and bonuses. I had five weeks of vacation. I was living comfortably. Knowing that I was going to start my own business pretty much from the ground up, my fear was, "Can I continue my lifestyle and make ends meet?" I knew I wasn't going to have that six figure salary initially.

You also asked me if that fear been realized or have I gotten past it. I had an opportunity come up with *Comcast*, after I left *Verizon*, which would have led to a position with the same structure as I previously had. I told myself, "You know, spending these past nine months without a paycheck and realizing that we could cut back on a lot of things, that I really don't need to live like this. There are things I can cut back on. There are things I can do smarter and live better with less." My goal within five years was to be where I was with *Verizon* financially, and then within ten years to have equity in the business to sell or reinvest. I realized that I didn't have that opportunity at *Verizon*. I had a nice salary. I had a nice 401k. I had nice bonuses, but at the end of the day when I left, that's all I had. I had no equity. Hopefully one day I will ask myself, "Okay, do I resign my contract with *CertaPro Painters*, or do I start to look at my portfolio or selling my business? What equity do I get from that?"

Q. What was the best advice you received while you were investigating your franchise purchase?

A. Some of the best advice I received was when I was talking to other *CertaPro Painters* franchisees. They told me, "You need to make sure you've got support because once you sign that contract, you are pretty much on your own. It is now your business." With *CertaPro Painters*, I have gotten that support.

Q. How did you go about funding your franchise?

A. I was fortunate in that with my position at *Verizon*, I had an executive buyout. I also had restricted stock and performance stock payments that I had gotten over the years. I will still get payments because they are vested, and the payout is usually three years in arrears. I also have a 401k. I did a combination of things to fund the franchise. I established a new IRA 401k because I had to roll it over since I was no longer at *Verizon*. I used that IRA to take a loan out to fund a portion of my franchise purchase. I also used personal savings and my stock payments were another portion of it.

Q. What was the biggest challenge you have had in building your business? Did you anticipate this challenge? Do you believe you have overcome it?

A. The biggest challenge for me was staffing and scaling the business. When do I do it? How do I do it? What's the right way to do it? I feel I have overcome the staffing issue because I have a full bench of painters, even more than I currently need. Other challenges I now face concern me doing all the operational tasks for the business. I do almost everything in that regard. I have a part-time office assistant that comes in one day a week that helps with the accounting functions, which is helpful. I am starting now to wonder when I should hire a sales manager or a residential account manager. Someone who can take on a portion of the business that I am now doing so I can scale my business into more commercial projects. I am wondering how do I do that, and how do I make sure I have enough cash flow to pay for that person, and what do I do from a performance measurement perspective? These are the challenges I am now facing.

Q. Where do you see yourself and your business five years from now?

A. Beyond the equity I've established in the business and the ability I would have to sell it, the one thing that would keep me interested in staying in the business is to be the ideal boss. To be the owner of a business that employs people and gives them some security in a job that treats them fairly and helps them provide for their family. I'd like to have a business that positively contributes to the community where I live. I often think about getting more work so I can keep my employees working. Today they are almost living pay check to pay check. I have had a painter come up to me, thank me and say, "I can't tell you how happy I am that you gave me an opportunity to paint for you. My house was in foreclosure. I was literally losing my home and now you have given me a second chance." I would love to build the business where I have sales people, full-time office support, painters on staff, and where we are all working together. I'd like to have holiday parties, community events, and a store front in the community. That's where I'd like to see my business grow.

> "Knowing that I was going to start my own business pretty much from the ground up, my fear was, 'Can I continue my lifestyle and make ends meet?' I knew I wasn't going to have that six figure salary initially."

Q. Are you having fun? Are you making money? Would you do it again?

A. Am I having fun? Yes. I often say that I would prefer to be a professional athlete or a self-made millionaire, because I think that would be really fun, but that's not happening. The business is fun because I get to meet different people every single day. Every house I go into, every commercial customer I meet, they have a different story. Part of the fun that comes from my business is that I've got two boys that are playing football. When they were younger and were in soccer, I missed a lot of their games. I've done things with them during the last year that I never did in the past. My philosophy at my corporate job was that I needed to be one of the first people who showed up for work in the morning and was one of the last people to leave at night. That was the corporate culture. I often didn't get home until 8:00 at night when they were being tucked into bed. I get to do things with my family that I didn't get to do before. That's the best part about this business.

Am I making money? I am making enough money now that we can continue the same lifestyle we currently have. I am not making enough money to live the lifestyle I used to live, which, in retrospect, was probably over the top. We are comfortable. We are happy.

Would I do it all over again? Unless it was forced upon me, probably not because I was comfortable at *Verizon*. I had been there my whole career. I was making good money. I was very successful at *Verizon*. If that model or that paradigm had not changed, I would probably still be there. I didn't hate my job. I didn't hate the people I worked for. But that business model changed and as a result of that change, I was forced to go look for other opportunities. Would I do a *CertaPro Painters* opportunity again? Absolutely.

"There is vitality, life force, energy that is translated through you into action, and because there is only one of you, your expression is unique. If you block it, it will never exist through any other medium and be lost forever. It is not your business to determine how good or valuable it compares with other expressions, it is your business to keep the channel open."

- Martha Graham

WAYPOINT

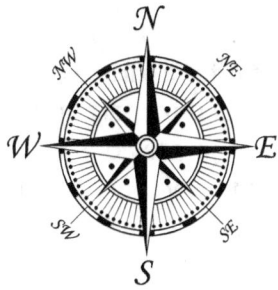

Advantages and Disadvantages of Franchising

To understand the advantages and disadvantages of owning a franchise business you need to have a basis for comparison. Other ways to realize your dreams through business ownership include buying a business opportunity and creating a business from the ground up. There are definite advantages and disadvantages to owing a franchise business over these other career or business ownership options but to know which path is right for you, you should first look at your motivations and qualifications for business ownership. Let's consider three scenarios:

Scenario One

You have been laid off from a 20-year career in banking. Even before the layoff, you realized you had reached the ceiling on your salary and possibilities for advancement in your career had diminished. Your company has given you a cash settlement and you are keen to take charge of your life, become your own boss and learn some new skills along the way. You want a good income and are willing to put in whatever hours necessary to jump start the new career but your overall goal is to eventually work reasonable hours and have more time for yourself and your family.

If your history is similar, you are probably an excellent candidate for franchise ownership. This path will allow you to benefit from a proven system of operations and a training program that will quickly get you up and running. As you have no previous business ownership experience, the ongoing support you will receive from a franchisor will be vital to your success. Many franchise opportunities offer a turnkey package that will include almost everything you need to start your business. In addition, most franchisors require no previous experience in their industry so you can be open to a variety of types of businesses and won't need to stick to the one industry you know. Franchisees can take advantage of lower cost materials due to group buying power. They also learn from each other and usually form a peer support system. Because you won't be occupied with every minute detail of owning a business as you begin down the path of franchising, you will be able to concentrate on growing your business.

One disadvantage to franchise ownership is that you must follow a franchisor's rules. In other words, you are in charge as long as you follow and adhere to all of the elements of the franchise system. This is necessary so that the franchisor can offer consistency across the brand — and let's face it, they've done the research and tested the procedures so their way is usually the right way. This is also a benefit to the consumer who can expect comparable quality products or services no matter which franchisee he patronizes, anywhere across the country or around the world.

The other perceived disadvantage is that a franchisee must pay royalties and sometimes a marketing fee to the franchisor. Royalty payments are compensation for everything the franchisor provides, including access to the brand, the operating system and related items. The franchisor uses the marketing fee to provide national advertising to build the brand and drive market penetration at a greater level than a franchisee could do on his own. Also, national marketing funds enable franchisees to benefit from professionally produced marketing materials and realize efficiencies from commingled funds.

Scenario Two

As a truly entrepreneurial individual, you are brimming with ideas for new products or businesses and love to "tinker" with things until they are just as you want them. You are strongly attracted to the idea of being your own boss and don't like the idea of answering to others. You have the drive to follow through on your plans and have a background in a variety of disciplines, including sales, marketing, accounting and management, so you are not looking for outside support. You have plenty of money to spend on researching and developing your product/service so a predictable timeframe for break even isn't a concern.

If you are like this type of person, one who likes blazing his own trails, franchise ownership is not for you. Instead you will be more comfortable setting up your own business using your own ideas. This is the most risky way to become your own boss because you will not have the proven operations system, nationwide brand and marketing, and the ongoing support of a franchise company. You may also have more difficulty obtaining business loans and the time from inception to when you start turning a profit will be hard to predict. On the plus side, you will owe no royalties and can run you business just as you please. Historically this is the model least likely to succeed on average so it is recommended only for truly exceptional individuals who have the desire and stamina to start their own business based on their own unique idea or approach.

Scenario Three

A varied work history has given you some great skills which you wish to put to use running your own business. You are not concerned about the type of business you buy but want to have freedom to run it your way. You would be okay with a certain degree of risk but also recognize the advantages of an established system of operations. Although you don't have a lot of cash to invest, your spouse works so you will have income for the time it takes your business to begin making money.

If you're the type of person who will never stop and ask directions, a business opportunity may be the right type of business for you. This is a business you buy outright and have the freedom to run your own way. The benefit of a business opportunity is that they generally provide you with a successful business model and possibly some training and marketing assistance. Marketing assistance and training, however, may be under developed or nonexistent. The initial investment is usually lower than for a franchise and there are no ongoing royalty payments.

A downside to business opportunities is that the seller isn't invested in your success or failure because he makes all of his money up front. Therefore, you won't have extensive ongoing training, assistance, a national marketing program, research and development, etc. The risk factor is probably greater than for owning a franchise but could be less than starting your own business.

Franchising is a Better Way

For a majority of people, franchising has proven to be a viable way to become a business owner. For the most part it offers the lowest risks and the highest level of support. Because a franchisor doesn't succeed until the franchisees do, you'll find a team of dedicated professionals willing and able to help you every step of the way, from site selection to employee hiring to grand opening. They will keep in touch with you from the very beginning to years down the road and they have web sites, toll free numbers and a dedicated staff to make sure all your questions are answered quickly. The cost of this continued support is usually in the form of royalty payments based on earnings but most franchisees feel the benefits are worth the expense. Research and development is possible because of feedback from those in the field and this cooperative involvement is a hallmark of a well-run franchise business.

The final benefit of franchising is that you buy a package – product or service, brand name and trademarks, marketing and advertising, operations manuals and proven systems – along with thorough training in every aspect of the business. You can totally change careers without years of schooling or apprenticeship or research. One day you can have a "job" as accountant or police officer and a few months later have a "career" as the successful owner of a business, which may be an auto detailer or a pet spa or a home improvement franchise.

And that's why franchising succeeds – because it works, for the franchisor, for the franchisee and for the consumer.

Business Ownership Comparisons	Franchise	Business Opportunity	Your Own Business
Potential Risk Factor	Lower	Moderate	High
Cost	Moderate to High	Usually Moderate	Whatever You Want to Spend
Training	Yes	Possibly	None
Proven Operating System	Yes	Yes	No
Ongoing Support	Yes	No	No
Royalty Payments	Yes	No	No
Upfront Fee	Yes	Yes	No
Brand Name Recognition	Yes	Maybe	No
National Marketing Fund	Yes	No	No
Marketing Help	Yes	Maybe	No
Group Buying Power	Yes	Maybe	No
FDD Provided	Yes	No	No

"You gain strength, courage and confidence by every experience in which you really stop to look fear in the face. You must do the thing you think you cannot do."

- Eleanor Roosevelt

8

Dean & Kristin Moran, Synergy HomeCare

BACKGROUND

Kristin & Dean Moran opened their franchise, *Synergy HomeCare (Synergy)*, in August of 2008. Previously, Dean spent 17 years in the financial industry, serving as a senior vice president for a major bank, while Kristin was a stay-at-home mom for 12 years. They both decided to pursue a passion for opening their own business together.

The homecare industry came to them after they had watched their own grandparents age and their evolving needs to stay at home. Kristin and Dean are parents of four children, one with Type 1 diabetes. Dean is an active board member of the *Juvenile Diabetes Research Foundation* and Kristin serves on the board of her local community resource council; helping others in need is a passion they both share. When not working, they can be found cheering their children on at a hockey rink or soccer field.

INTERVIEW

Q. What franchise did you purchase and when?
A. We purchased a *Synergy* franchise and we opened our doors August of 2008.

Q. When was this company founded and how many existing franchisees are there in the system?
A. It was founded in the mid to late '90's by Peter Torian. He started up his own home care agency after retiring from the police force in Arizona. He started franchising right around 2000. To date, we are in 32 states with over 800 franchises.

Q. What were you doing for work prior to you opening your franchise?
A. Kristen was a stay-at-home mom for our 4 children for 12 years, and I was a senior vice president for *JP Morgan Chase*.

Q. Had you ever run a business before your opening your franchise? How has the transition been from a corporate career to running your own business?
A. This is the first business that we have owned and operated ourselves. When I was with *Chase*, I was running a very large division. So being involved in the planning and strategizing as well as managing the profit & loss have definitely helped us here. Being out on your own is a much more rewarding type of work than it was working for a corporation because each and every day you recognize that the effort you put into the day is going to contribute directly to the bottom line. There's really a vast difference between being self employed and working for a corporation.

Q. What was the precipitator that got you guys thinking that it was time for you to do something different, and started looking into having your own business?
A. It was kind of the merger of a couple of different things that were going on at the same time. For me, I was in the financial industry and obviously the economy during the past few years has not been good. I was asked to let go many people at *Chase* and that really just left me in unrest about my career with everything that was going on over there. At the same exact time my wife was really starting to step out and start looking at business opportunities after our four kids were in

school. She was really the first one who had the impressions of being self-employed. She and I have been together since we were 18 years old and it was just something that we wanted to do together.

> *"For someone who is considering getting into a franchise or any business that they own, unless you are willing to jump in feet first, you probably shouldn't do it."*

So I walked away from the corporate world and we teamed up and that's how we got involved.

Q. What attracted you to the franchise concept as opposed to starting up a business on your own?

A. Fortunately for me, I came across a gentleman who was a franchise broker. He really outlined what our strengths and attributes were, as well as what made us feel good about the work we do. He came back to us with a narrowed down list of industries. Both my wife and I were heavily influenced by our grandparents. We were very close to our grandparents, so this particular industry fit like a glove. What really won us over as far as *Synergy* goes, was one of our sons is a special needs child and this is pretty much the only franchise that services clients of all ages. We have been very involved in the research for the cure for his disease and this was really just an extension of what we had going on in our private life.

Q. Did you consider other franchises in your search?

A. We did. We looked at some of the competition that was in the home care industry, along with business coaching businesses. Kris was initially attracted to businesses in the coffee industry.

Q. What attracted you to the franchise you now run and how did you determine this was the best franchise for you?

A. The owner of *Synergy* left a career in law enforcement by choice. When I first started visiting with them, they exuded a level of passion that I think my wife and I knew we'd bring to the table as well. In addition, it's a family run corporation. The owner has his brother involved and it feels very warm when you walk through the door of the corporate headquarters. With the other businesses we investigated, I got the impression that they were more about selling a franchise versus being completely concerned and immersed with your success and making sure that you are put on a path of success.

Q. You mentioned earlier about working with a franchise broker. Tell me about that process?

A. Yes, we worked with a franchise consultant in our investigation. I never, ever would have thought of this industry on my own, to be honest with you. I didn't even really know it existed. My career has always been one of financial services. When we met with the consultant he really talked to us about our strengths and our weaknesses, what our earnings had been for the past few years, and our personal income. He also asked about our likes and dislikes. I can be completely honest and say that if it wasn't for him, we wouldn't have gotten into this business because we really didn't know anything about it.

Q. What was your biggest fear in deciding to purchase your franchise, how did you get over it, and was this fear ever realized?

A. Our fear concerned the amount of territory we would be purchasing and the amount of time we would be spending in the business. We have a big family, so we wondered if we would be able to wear all the hats that we needed in order to make our business succeed. We wanted to succeed without taking time away from our four children and our family life and all that it en-

> *"We used personal savings and 401k money. We leveraged our family's future."*

tails. It's definitely tough. For someone who is considering getting into a franchise or any business that they own, unless you are willing to jump in feet first, you probably shouldn't do it. Our kids have been great. They have sacrificed a lot and they know just as much about this business as we do. It's part of our conversations and we just crossed the two year mark this month and we have definitely come a long, long way. Our business now is quite profitable. I think my wife would agree that we feel much surer about our future from when we first set out to do this.

Q. What was the best advice you received while you were investigating your franchise purchase?
A. The best advice I received was to make sure that I fully researched the business and to make sure I was aware of both the pros and the cons, the dangers. I was told to evaluate the risk versus the investment and most importantly, the one thing the franchise broker told me, is if you don't love it, don't do it. Unless it's your heart that tells you each and every day that you are happy going to work and you are doing what you love to do, then you most likely will not do well. That for me was probably the key thing.

Q. Do you feel that you have received adequate support from your franchise parent in growing the business and are there any areas for improvement?
A. Yes. I do feel we have had a lot of support through the corporate offices. I think sometimes we could have used a little more support, but when we opened our franchise in 2008, *Synergy* was still pretty new at the franchising system. They have recently hired some quality, key people that have definitely stepped up to the plate to help the new owners.

Q. How did you go about funding your franchise?
A. We used our own personal assets. We bought a large amount of territory because that's basically how our business works best. It's based on geographic area. Although we were very

nervous about it, we bought a lot of territory because we wanted to be prepared for future growth. We really didn't want to be hamstrung because we didn't buy enough up front. We knew that this was going to be a hot business in our industry and that the rest of the territory around us would sell out. We used personal savings and 401k money. We leveraged our family's future. It was a very large investment for us up front.

Q. What has been the biggest challenge you have had in building your business? Did you anticipate this challenge and do you feel you have overcome it?

A. On the sales end of it, it was initially very hard because this is absolutely a 100% referral based business. If you are not comfortable with representing yourself and your company and networking and exuding confidence, then you are probably not going to do well. At the end of the day, you are your own brand. I have seen owners who, right out of the gate, have tried to go out and hire marketers to do it for them, but that strategy to me just doesn't work. People need to know and see the owner. So in this particular industry if they like you and they trust you, then they will definitely do business with you. Another one of the main challenges was just learning how to deal with the different types of people in this industry. You are dealing with your hourly wage workers, and you are dealing with the families, and you are dealing with the referral sources. You have to wear a bunch of different hats and know how to talk to each and every one of them. You need to make sure that your business is professional, but you are also coming through as being empathetic and sympathetic to their needs. You have to let them know that you really do care about their needs and that you are there to help them.

Q. Where do you see yourself and your business five years from now?

A. We obviously do want to grow our business. We want to be

able to bring in more people to help us. I really enjoy being involved in charity work and things of that nature. I am on the board of directors for my son's foundation and I really want our company to be different than all the other home care businesses. Together we want our company to be involved in charitable work and really be a part of the fabric of the community. We want to be different and we want to be recognized as an industry expert. We want families to be able to come to us not just for service, but also for advice. There are a lot of people out there that don't need our service but certainly need our advice. Doing lectures and seminars and things of that nature are really important for me.

Q. Are you having fun, are you making money, and would you do it again?

A. Yes, we are having a fun. We are making money, and I would do it again. We definitely would do another franchise. We got through the last two years and I know that we are going to be growing and we are going to be able to take off some of the hats we are wearing. The things that are difficult and challenging for us each and every day, the further out we go in this business, the less of it we are personally going to be doing as owners. I would definitely do it again. It's very challenging, but it is very rewarding especially when you are helping out a patient. I would definitely do it again, for sure.

"You will become as small as your controlling desire, or as great as your dominant aspiration."

- James Allen

9

Craig Radice, Pooch-Mobile

BACKGROUND

At the time of this interview, Craig has been married for 17 years with two teenage girls. He's a 16 year corporate graduate in telecommunications with a background in information technology and business process reengineering. Craig moved to Colorado and started a new life as a franchisee in mobile dog washing.

INTERVIEW

Q. What franchise did you purchase and when?

A. I bought *The Pooch Mobile* franchise. It originated in Australia. I bought it in March of 2006.

Q. When was this company founded and how many existing franchisees are there currently in the system that you are aware of?

A. The company was founded by Chris Taylor in 1991. There are franchisees in Australia, New Zealand, New Caledonia, Malaysia, England, and now in the United States. I believe there's a total of 235 current franchisees.

Q. What were you doing for work prior to opening your franchise?
A. The majority of my career was spent in a corporate environment. I spent 16 years at a fortune 50 company working in telecommunications until I got laid off. After that I managed multi-million dollar material handling projects. I ultimately said good-bye to that job and lifestyle because I was always gone working for them and not for myself.

Q. Had you ever run your own business before opening the franchise? How was the transition for you?
A. I had never ran a business before opening this franchise. The transition was a shock. In running your own business you are responsible for all the income generation, all the operations, all of the accounting and marketing. In a corporate environment, you basically have a title and specific job responsibilities and you get paid every week.

Q. What attracted you to the franchise concept as opposed to starting up a business entirely on your own?
A. To sum it up, a franchise is a business in a box. With a franchise you are purchasing a name, processes, procedures, and a proven business model. In starting up a business on your own, you have to do a lot of research and due diligence on your own. The franchise concept offers you an opportunity to hit the ground running.

Q. Did you consider other franchises in your search?
A. I did consider other ones. One was a business which dealt with foundational cracks. Another one was a stain glass overlay company which dealt with creating a kind of inexpensive stain glass façade for people. A final one was a business for installing auto accessories.

Q. What attracted you to the franchise you now run and how did you determine this was the best franchise for you?
A. I was attracted to the industry. I looked at the animal care

industry as a growing trend and the forecasted growth was significant, versus the other industries that I was considering. I did a risk reward quadrant analysis looking at the pet industry. It turned out that it was a $38 billion dollar industry at the time. Now I think it is $53 billion industry, so it's basically on an upward growth.

Q. Did you work on your own to find your franchise?
A. I did not work on my own to find a franchise. I ran into someone who recommended a franchise consultant, Stephen Hogan, to my wife. I never knew this type of person existed and after about 30 days of hemming and hawing, I finally called him. I thought he was basically just going to try to sell me anything, but it turned out to be a good relationship. I felt comfortable and he really understood me and took the time to understand what my criteria was as far as my attributes, what my desires were, and match those with franchises he felt would be a good fit for me.

> *"The franchise concept offers you an opportunity to hit the ground running."*

Q. What was your biggest fear in deciding to purchase your franchise and how did you get over it? Was this fear every realized?
A. My biggest fear was basically giving someone a lot of money and not knowing if I was going to get it back. I decided to just go for it. I found that some encouragement and coaching from Stephen Hogan helped, along with the due diligence process in investigating the franchises. Talking with my wife and my family, and reviewing all of the information that I received, enabled me to build some confidence and make the decision to buy the franchise.

Q. What was the best advice you received while you were investigating your franchise purchase?

A. The best advice I received was that there's a lot of franchise businesses out there and not all of them are good ones. You've got to be careful with the franchise you buy because there can be failures at the corporate level and I have seen this happen. The organization that Stephen Hogan is affiliated with works only with highly qualified franchise businesses. Those businesses had to meet a certain criteria and have some credibility behind them, which was important to me.

> *"It has been great being out and about, meeting people, being involved in the community, and building a business and not having to go to the corporate desk."*

Q. Do you feel you have received adequate support from your franchise parent in growing your business?
A. As far as adequate support, yes. They know the business and have a fundamental interest in building the franchise organization. They are available through voicemail, email, as well as in person to meet and to check or review things.

Q. How did you go about funding your franchise?
A. We purchased it through a lump sum payment from our personal savings.

Q. What is the biggest challenge you have had in building your business and did you anticipate this challenge? How have you overcome it?
A. The biggest challenge has been enough time to do all the different roles within the business and wearing many hats. Did I anticipate the challenge? Not really. I guess it's kind of like having a child. You think you are going to have a child and that you are going to have plenty of time to continue doing other things, and then you realize that a child consumes just about all of your time. That's really what a business does when you are growing it. I've overcome it by taking deep

breaths, taking it easy, and just rolling with it. I've learned to be flexible and not to get too stressed out because I can always continue working on it the next day.

Q. Where do you see yourself and your business five years from now?
A: I can see myself selling this business.

Q. Are you having fun, are you making money, and would you do it again?
A. Yes, it's been fun. It has been great being out and about, meeting people, being involved in the community, and building a business and not having to go to the corporate desk. Am I making money? Yes. It's definitely a good business that I am in. Would I do it again? Looking back, it has been a successful venture. I would say that my decision to buy *The Pooch Mobile* was the right decision for me.

"It is better to follow the voice inside and be at war with the whole world, than to follow the ways of the world and be at war with your deepest self."

- Michael Pastore

10

Matt Swope, Heaven's Best Carpet Cleaning

BACKGROUND
At the time of this interview, Matt is 31 and has been married for 9 years with 2 kids. Matt has been in business for 8 years and lives in Fort Collins, Colorado. Fort Collins is where Matt has been fortunate enough to call home for most of his life.

INTERVIEW
Q. What franchise did you purchase and when?
A. I purchased a *Heaven's Best Carpet Cleaning* franchise. The purchase was in 2002.

Q. When was Heaven's Best as a company founded and how many existing franchisees are there in the system?
A. It was originally founded in 1983. I believe there are about 450 different franchisees throughout the US, Canada, and England.

Q. What were you doing for work prior to opening your franchise?
A. I was working for my dad before I bought it. I bought the business from my parents, so I was working for him before that.

Q. If you had only had corporate jobs, or just the experience of working for your dad, how has the transition been from an employee to a business owner?

A. It was really easy for me. Most of the customers already knew me and knew that I was the son of the previous owner, so that transition went very well. I didn't get anybody that complained about my dad not being in the business anymore because they had already worked with me before. It was a very easy transition for me.

Q. What attracted you to the franchise concept as opposed to starting up your own business?

A. I saw my dad running the business and he wasn't really a business guy. His motto was basically, "Do a good job and people will call you back." I thought, "Well, if he can do it, I can do it," and that's what I did.

Q. Did you consider other franchises in your search? If so which ones?

A. I don't think my dad thought about any other concepts or companies. We were in Nebraska at the time and my dad was working at a ranch there. It just wasn't working out for him. One of our friends suggested to my father that he clean carpets. My dad just kind of laughed at him and said, "Yeah right." Long story short, we moved from Nebraska to Fort Collins and he started Heaven's Best Carpet Cleaning. For me, as far as deciding to buy it, I just told him I would do it. My dad did a lot of the leg work and a lot of the start-up stuff. I just continued what he was doing, just on bigger scale.

Q. How did your dad come to find out about *Heaven's Best*? Did he work with someone to find it?

A. My dad's friend worked with *Heaven's Best Carpet Cleaning*. He was actually the state owner for Nebraska and the area he worked in was North Platt, Nebraska. The friend was a Heaven's Best franchisee and a state owner. He was the one that introduced us to *Heaven's Best*.

Q. What was your biggest fear in deciding to purchase your dad's franchise and how did you get over it?

A. I didn't really have a big fear. Over the years I got to know the owner of *Heaven's Best*, Cody Howard. I met him when I was younger when my parents were running the business. When I bought it, it was just me and a van and one employee. There really wasn't anything else to do differently. I just kept on doing what my parents were doing because I knew it worked. I did start advertising more. When I first took over the business, I didn't have a whole lot of overhead to support. I had extra funds to try different things as far as advertising went and figured out what worked and what didn't.

> *"I saw my dad running the business and he wasn't really a business guy. His motto was basically, "Do a good job and people will call you back." I thought, "Well, if he can do it, I can do it," and that's what I did."*

Q. What was the best advice you received while you were investigating your franchise purchase?

A. My dad just said, "Do a good job and you will succeed." He also said, "*Heaven's Best* has done their part, and as long as you do a good job you will be successful." I remember him specifically saying that.

Q. Do you feel you have received adequate support from your franchise parent in growing your business? What are some areas for improvement, if any?

A. *Heaven's Best* supports us very well. Cody Howard still owns the business that he started in 1983. I can almost always get a hold of him the same day I call. If he is in the middle of training some people, it might take a little longer. His vice president, John, has been with the company ever since there was that position, so he knows a lot about it. The one area for improvement is a small item. In my opinion, I think they jump too quickly into using a new product before they are really tested out. They basically get a product out to different franchisees and say, "Here's a new product we are trying out. Try it out...this is what it does...this is how you use it... give us feedback."

Q. How did you go about funding your franchise?

A. We tried to go through a bank, but being that there's so much blue sky in a service business, we found that avenue was difficult. There isn't a lot of collateral in our business, either. My parents decided to finance the whole thing for us, which was wonderful. I pay them a percentage of whatever the business pulls in each month. In a good month, I paid them a lot. In a month where sales were less, I made hardly anything. I just kept on paying that percentage until the loan was paid off. It took about five years.

Q. What was the biggest challenge you had in building your business?

A. I have probably doubled the business since my parents had it. My biggest challenge now is hiring the right people and training them to the way we do our business and instilling in them to be as picky as I would be.

Q. Where do you see yourself and your business five years from now?

A. I probably will sell it five years from now. I don't really have any specific plans. I have thought about it, but life's too short to clean carpet all my life. So either that, or have somebody run it for me while I do something else.

Q. Are you having fun, are you making money, and would you do it again?

A. Yes, I would do it again. There are some things I would do differently, but yes I would go into this type of franchise again. I am having fun and yes, I am making money. I am still young so I don't take enough vacation time, but my theory is to work hard now, while you can, so you don't have to work hard later. It's been very fun.

CONCLUSION

First Steps
What to do <u>before</u> you search for a franchise

The lure of franchise ownership can be a heady experience. You imagine the thrill of being your own boss, creating wealth for yourself instead of someone else. But you don't want to enter the search process unprepared, susceptible to mistakes.

You have so many questions: Will you be happy as a franchisee? Can you make the money you need to provide for yourself and your future? Where do you even start, with thousands of franchise opportunities available?

The best way to beat the odds, even before you even begin looking at franchises, is to do an introspective self-evaluation of your own strengths and challenges. So, sit down, get out paper and pen, and as objectively as possible answer these questions:

SKILLS / STRENGTHS

- What part of your current and past jobs have you liked doing the most?
- List your skills and evaluate how well you perform each.
- How focused will you be on customer service?
- Are you already an active part of your community or will you be actively networking to build your business?
- Describe the work environment that most appeals to you, such as busy mall location, home office or quiet industrial space.
- Do you have a background in sales or marketing? Do you enjoy cold calling or do you prefer that customers come to you?
- Are you status conscious? Does it matter to you what the product or service of the franchise is or does the business potential matter more?

CHALLENGES

- What part of your current and past jobs have you liked doing the least?
- List your weakness, those things you'd not want to do or would want to hire someone to do in a business.

MANAGEMENT SKILLS

- Do you have any experience managing employees? Do you enjoy managing people? What type of employee would you most enjoy working with (skilled, minimum wage, etc.) and what number of employees would you be comfortable managing?
- How do you feel about recruiting employees?
- Do you have the experience and skill needed to create a work environment that will allow you to retain employees?

FINANCIAL CONSIDERATIONS

- How much capital do you have to invest?
- Can you afford to do without a regular income during the start-up phase of your new business?
- What are your financial goals?
- How do you see your lifestyle changing as a result of meeting your financial goals?
- How do you feel about taking the risk of becoming self-employed?

ARE YOU A TEAM PLAYER?

- Franchising is all about following someone else's system. Can you picture yourself in this role, executing a system you didn't create?

Once you have answered these questions, you'll begin to see a clearer picture of what talents you can bring to a franchise business and what you expect to receive in return. The next step is to start looking at opportunities and evaluating them based on your answers. It may take some effort to find the right franchise but don't compromise on your goals.

If you need help, a franchise consultant company such as FranChoice can offer you guidance and suggest businesses that will fit you whatever your goals and desires for business ownership may be.

Franchise opportunities come in many shapes and sizes and you never need to settle for one that is just not a great fit. Choosing the franchise opportunity that best matches your needs, interests and style is your greatest assurance of happiness and success.

ABOUT THE AUTHOR

Leslie Lautzenhiser is the co-owner of *PuroClean Restoration Services, Inc.*, a franchised water/mold/fire damage restoration business in Fort Collins, Colorado. She is also a franchise consultant working with both individuals who are interested in buying a franchise as well as businesses who are interested in franchising. She is also a Manager with *Fortune High Tech Marketing*, a direct selling business and works in Business Development for *HRAnswerLink*. She is active with the Fort Collins *Junior League* and is on the steering committee of the Fort Collins *Quid Novi Festival*, which connects and educates writers, inventors and entrepreneurs. She is married with two children, Rachel and Ryan and loves writing, fishing and spending time in the mountains with her family. She holds a Bachelor's Degree in Journalism and a Masters Degree in Human Resources Management.

Stay connected with Leslie and learn about her next volume at: http://franchises.50interviews.com

Or to learn more about Franchoice, visit: http://www.franchoice.com/llautzenhiser

ABOUT 50 INTERVIEWS

50 Interviews is a publisher of books, CDs, videos, and software that serve to inform, educate, and inspire others on a wide range of topics. Timely insight, inspiration, collective wisdom, and best practices derived directly from those who have already succeeded. Authors surround themselves with those they admire, gain clarity of purpose, adopt critical beliefs, and build a network of peers to ensure success in that endeavor. Readers gain knowledge and perspective from those who have already achieved a result they desire.

Imagine a university where not only does each student get a textbook custom tailored to a curriculum they personally designed, but where each student literally becomes the author!

The mission of 50 Interviews is to provide aspiring, passionate, driven people a framework to achieve their dreams of becoming that which they aspire to be. Learning what it takes to be the best in your field; directly from those who have already succeeded. The ideal author is someone who desires to be a recognized expert in their field. You will be part of a community of authors who share your passion and who have learned firsthand how the **50 Interviews** concept works. A form of extreme education, the process promises to transform you into that which you aspire to become.

If you are interested in learning more, I would love to hear from you! You can contact me via email at: brian@50interviews.com, by phone: 970-215-1078 (Colorado), or through our website:

www.50interviews.com

All my best,
Brian Schwartz
Creator of **50 Interviews**

OTHER 50 INTERVIEWS TITLES

Additional topics based on the *50 Interviews* model that have already been released or are in development:

Athletes Over 50
by Don McGrath, Ph.D.

Young Entrepreneurs
by Nick Tart

Attraction Marketers
by Rob Christensen

Scientists
by David Giltner, Ph.D.

Physicians in Transition
by Rich Fernandez, MD

Property Managers
by Michael Levy

Professional Speakers
by Laura Lee Carter and Brian Schwartz

Successful Jobseekers
by Gordon Nuttall

Video Marketers
by Randy Berry

Spiritualists
by Tuula Fai

Financial Planners
by Allen Duck

Entrepreneurs
by Brian Schwartz

Women Millionaires
by Kirsten McCay-Smith

And many more...

Learn more at
www.50interviews.com

www.ingramcontent.com/pod-product-compliance
Lightning Source LLC
Chambersburg PA
CBHW052106070526
44584CB00017B/2354